DATE DUE

~~June~~			

The Library Store   #47-0103

Ancient
WEST AFRICAN KINGDOMS

Revised and Updated

JANE SHUTER

Heinemann Library
Chicago, Illinois

Photo research by Mica Brancic
Designed by Richard Parker and Manhattan Design
Printed and bound in China by CTPS

13 12 11 10 09
10 9 8 7 6 5 4 3 2 1

New edition ISBNs: 978-1-4329-1332-8 (hardcover)
                     978-1-4329-1340-3 (paperback)

Acknowledgments
The author and publishers are grateful to the following for permission to reproduce photographs: p. 7 © Werner Forman Archive/L. Entwistle Collection; p. 9 © The Detroit Institute of Arts; p. 11 © The University of Iowa Museum of Art, The Stanley Collection (1986.490); p. 12 © Photograph by Franko Khoury/National Museum of African Art, Smithsonian Institution; p. 13 © Giraudon/Art Resouce, NY; p. 16 © Getty Images/Lonely Planet Images; p. 17 © Getty Images/Gallo Images/Travel Ink; p. 18 © Michael Kirtley/National Geographic Society Image Collection; p. 19 © Mary Evans Picture Library; pp. 22, 23, 29 © Wolfgang Kaehler; p. 24 © The University of Iowa Museum of Art, The Stanley Collection (1986.451); p. 25 © Getty Images/Photographer's Choice/Gavin Hellier; pp. 26, 30 © Georg Gerster/Photo Researchers, Inc.; p. 28 © Thomas A. Hale, Pennsylvania State University.

Illustrations: p. 4 Eileen Mueller Neill; pp. 15, 21, 27 Juvenal "Marty" Martinez.
Cover photograph courtesy of © akg-images/André Held.

Every effort has been made to contact copyright holders of any material reproduced in this book. Any omissions will be rectified in subsequent printings if notice is given to the publisher.

Contents

Some words are shown in bold, **like this**.
You can find out what they mean by looking in the glossary.

Introduction

This map shows the kingdoms of Ghana, Mali, and Songhai, which ruled part of West Africa at different times between 700 and 1600.

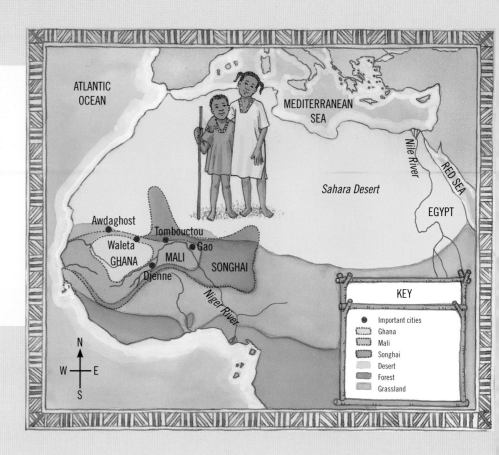

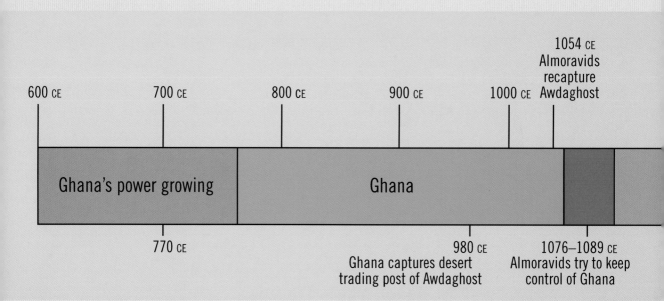

600 CE   700 CE   800 CE   900 CE   1000 CE

1054 CE
Almoravids recapture Awdaghost

Ghana's power growing

Ghana

770 CE

980 CE
Ghana captures desert trading post of Awdaghost

1076–1089 CE
Almoravids try to keep control of Ghana

For hundreds of years, West Africa was made up of different kingdoms. These kingdoms all had different languages and cultures. Their people's daily lives were similar, though, because they all had the same weather and landscape. They farmed the same kinds of crops in the same ways. They all lived a mostly outdoor life.

Between 770 and 1591, three different kingdoms rose one after another to become the most important kingdoms in West Africa. They were the kingdoms of Ghana, Mali, and Songhai. They each became powerful because they traded with the kingdoms on the other side of the Sahara Desert.

The three kingdoms fell for similar reasons. They became too big and their rulers could not keep control. They used their power to make trade unfair for those with whom they traded. Angry groups from the other side of the desert invaded both Ghana and Songhai.

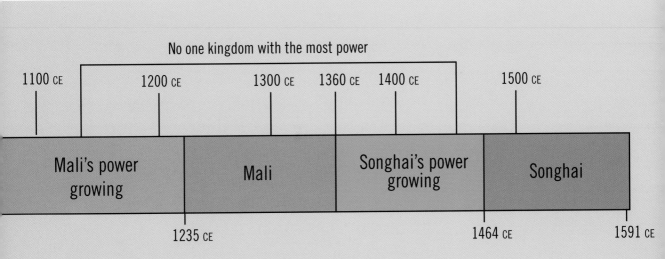

Ghana

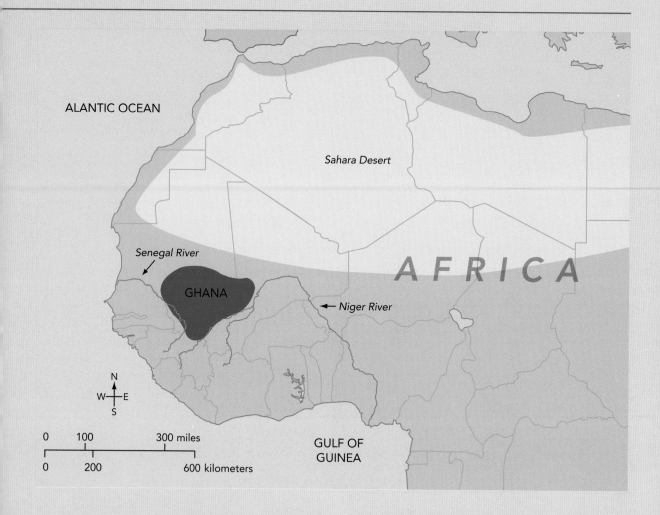

ALANTIC OCEAN

Sahara Desert

Senegal River

GHANA

AFRICA

← Niger River

N
W—E
S

0   100   300 miles

0   200   600 kilometers

GULF OF
GUINEA

People lived in Ghana as far back as the year 300. They were one of many groups living in West Africa. Ghana had a huge advantage over the other groups because it was on the edge of the Sahara Desert. By about 770, the kings of Ghana had control of the trade routes to the Sahara. Anyone who wanted to trade with the people of the desert had to pay a tax to the king of Ghana for using these routes. This is when most people see the kingdom of Ghana as beginning.

The desert trade was based on a system of being fair. But the kings of Ghana became greedy. When they took over the trading post of Awdaghost, which had been controlled by the North African Almoravids, the kings of Ghana became too powerful. In 1054, the Almoravids attacked and took Awdaghost back.

Over the next 20 years, the Almoravids took over more and more of Ghana. It was hard for them to control the kingdom because they were not West Africans themselves. Ghana soon broke up into several small kingdoms.

The Akan people began to settle in Ghana after the kingdom broke up. This clay head probably represents an Akan king.

Mali

King Sundiata Keita and the people of Kangaba formed the kingdom of Mali, which was one of the kingdoms of Ghana. The kingdom of Mali started in the same place as the kingdom of Ghana.

King Sundiata Keita was Mali's first king. He became king in 1235. He had a strong army, which he used to take over other nearby kingdoms. Soon Mali grew bigger and took control of trade routes across the Sahara Desert. Control of the trade routes made Mali richer and more powerful.

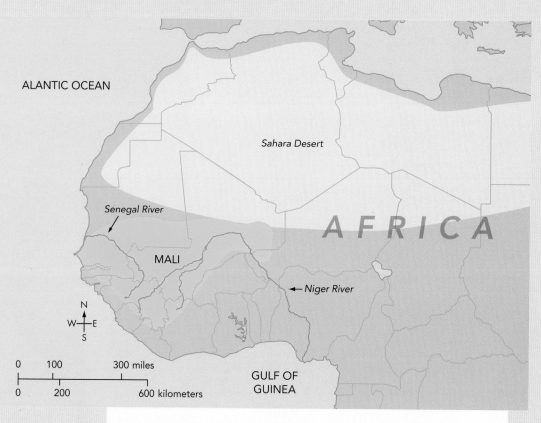

This map shows the kingdom of Mali at its largest, in about 1300.

By 1300, the kingdom of Mali was more than twice the size of the old kingdom of Ghana and had about twice as many people living in it. It was rich, peaceful, and had good rulers. But Mali had become too big. It had taken over too many different kingdoms.

These kingdoms all had different cultures, different languages, and their own royal families. They were not always happy to accept the king of Mali as their ruler. These people were quick to take advantage of a long argument over who should be the next king. Their kingdoms broke away and the kingdom of Mali collapsed. One of these "breakaway" kingdoms was the kingdom of Songhai.

West African sculptors who lived at this time used terra-cotta (baked clay) to make figurines.

Songhai

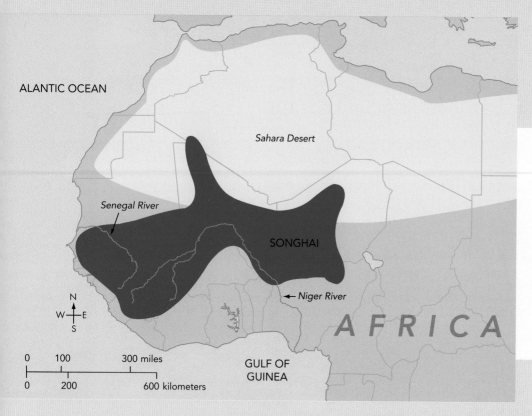

ALANTIC OCEAN

Sahara Desert

Senegal River

SONGHAI

N
W—E
S

← Niger River

AFRICA

0   100   300 miles
0   200   600 kilometers

GULF OF
GUINEA

This map shows the kingdom of Songhai at its largest, in about 1490.

Songhai was one of the first kingdoms to break away when Mali's kings lost control. Because Songhai was located on the Niger River, the skills of its sailors were useful for trade.

King Sonni Ali ruled Songhai starting in 1464. He was a warrior king, who steadily took over lands that had once been part of the kingdom of Mali. By 1492, when Sonni Ali died, Songhai controlled a huge kingdom. It also controlled the important trade routes across the Sahara Desert.

Songhai was the biggest of the three great West African kingdoms. This made it hard to control. Askia Muhammad, who ruled after Sonni Ali, took over the salt trade as well as the gold trade. The desert people had always controlled the salt trade, which kept trade fair between the two groups. Now Songhai had too much power in trade, too.

In 1528, Askia Muhammad's sons took over Songhai from their father. There were quarrels over who should rule. The kingdom began to break up. In 1591, the desert people of Morocco invaded and Songhai fell apart.

This clay figurine shows two women embracing. Experts think they are mourning the death of a loved one.

How Were They Ruled?

West African rulers were often shown on horseback. This figurine shows Sundiata Keita, the "Lion King of Mali."

All of the West African kingdoms were ruled by kings who came from royal families. Many of them were so powerful that they were seen almost as gods. Different kingdoms had different rules about who should take over. In some places, sons took over from their fathers. In others, children of the king's sister took over.

Many times it was not clear who was the right person to take over. So it was easy for arguments to break out over who the next ruler should be.

Rulers lived in palaces, away from the people. They had other people run the kingdom for them. **Officials** of different levels of importance worked for most West African kings. The officials enforced laws, collected taxes, and made sure things ran smoothly. Songhai grew so large that it was divided into 12 areas. Each had its own governor and officials. Ghana, Mali, and Songhai all had large armies to guard the trade routes. The armies also kept control of the kingdom.

This Spanish map of North Africa shows a trader visiting a West African king named Mansa Musa. Mansa Musa is dressed in blue and wears a crown.

Trade

Trade was an important part of life in West Africa. Ghana, Mali, and Songhai became powerful because they controlled trading. Groups of people followed the trade routes across the Sahara Desert. Each group traded a variety of goods (things made or grown to trade or swap). However, salt and gold were the most important trade goods.

The West African kingdoms had a lot of gold, while the desert people controlled areas where salt could be mined. Traders also swapped copper, dried fruit, cowrie shells, and **slaves**.

The earliest traders did not meet each other to swap their goods. Instead, they used a system called "silent trade." Silent trade was an easy way for people who did not speak the same language to exchange goods. Later traders met at oases or at trading points set up along rivers to trade. They still swapped goods instead of using money.

The silent trade system was important to the people of North and West Africa. This diagram shows how it worked.

Desert traders would bring salt, spices, and other goods they wanted to trade to an oasis (green spot in the middle of a desert).

They would lay the goods out, beat the drums to call the West African traders, then leave.

West African traders would decide how much gold to give for the salt and spices. They would put the gold next to the things they wanted. They would beat the drums and leave.

The desert traders would return. If they thought the swap was fair, they would take the gold and leave. If not, they would leave it, bang the drums again, and leave.

The West Africans would come back. If the gold was gone, they would take the goods left behind. If the gold was still there, they would decide whether or not to give more. If so, they would add it and beat the drums. This would go on until everyone had finished trading.

Religion

The Dogon people of Mali still honor the dead with masked dances, just like their ancestors did.

The earliest West Africans believed in a powerful "creator god" who made the world but did not interfere in people's lives. They also believed in **spirits** that controlled nature and did interfere in daily life. People prayed or made **offerings** to these spirits to keep them happy. They believed their dead relatives could talk to these spirits in the spirit world, so they had to keep their relatives happy, too.

Some people, called **diviners**, were said to have strong links to the spirit world. They told people, or even whole villages, what kind of offerings they had to give and what **rituals** they had to do. Most rituals involved dancing and singing, and some of them took several days.

Many of the North African people who traded with the West Africans were **Muslim**. As silent trade moved on to personal trade, they brought their religious ideas with them. The kings of Mali became Muslims. They built Muslim **temples**, called **mosques**, in their cities. These cities became centers of Muslim religion and learning. One city, Tombouctou, was famous for its **university**.

While the kings and their **courts** changed their religion, most of their people did not. In the countryside, ordinary people still kept their old beliefs. They were much slower to change.

This mosque in Djenné, Mali, was built out of mud bricks in the traditional style.

Cities

West African cities were important centers for crafts and trade. Skilled craft workers, like this potter, still use many of the same methods today.

Most West Africans lived in large family groups in farming settlements. Starting in about 1000, cities began to grow where the kings lived with their families and **officials**. The cities became important as trading places. At first only local people traded in the cities. Later, foreign traders came there, too.

A West African king lived in a palace in a separate part of the city from everyone else. From time to time he allowed people to come to his palace and ask for favors. Most of the time his officials enforced the laws. The king did not have to do it himself.

Djenné, once called Djenné-Jeno, was one of the earliest cities. By the year 1000, there were about 10,000 people living there. (London, one of the biggest European cities, had 40,000 people living in it at the time.) Most of the people living in the city were craft workers. Each type of craft worker lived in a separate part of the city.

Tombouctou was founded in about 1100. Under the rule of the Songhai kings, it grew in size until there were thousands of people living there. It had a royal palace, many **mosques**, busy markets, and a famous **university**.

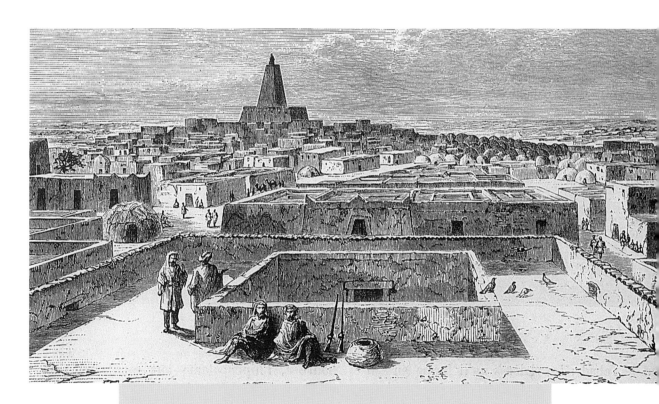

The city of Tombouctou became an important meeting place for people from all over West Africa. They traded goods as well as ideas.

Houses

Most people in West African kingdoms did not live in cities. They lived in villages in large family groups. Some villages were small, with less than 50 people living in them. Others were much larger. Villages had to be big enough so that all the people living there could make and grow everything the village needed.

Each village had a central circular **plaza** with "compounds" leading off from it. A compound was a group of huts around a central courtyard where much of the work was done. The chief of a village was expected to marry several women. He had a compound for each wife and at least one compound for his animals. Cattle were a sign of wealth, so a chief would hope to have lots of cattle. Less important people might only have one compound for everyone in the family and their animals.

This illustration shows a group of typical West African compounds.

Animals were brought into a fenced compound at night to keep them safe from wild animals that might want to eat them.

Grain was sometimes stored in raised storage bins that looked like small huts.

The doors of houses did not come all the way to the ground. A raised doorway made it harder for small animals to get in.

Each compound had its own fences.

Food and Farming

These men work together to prepare freshly harvested grain. They use the same process as people from the kingdoms of West Africa would have done.

West African farmers grew grains such as rice, millet, and sorghum, in addition to nuts and cotton. Farmers used simple hand tools, such as digging sticks and sickles, to dig the soil and **harvest** the crops. Because of the heat, the crops needed careful watering.

Farmers kept chickens for eggs and meat. They kept cows and goats for milk and meat. Merchants and important people kept horses and camels for transportation. The West African people used every part of the animals when they were killed. Feathers were used on clothes and masks. The fat was used for cooking, making candles, and softening dry skin.

Millet was the most important crop. It was ground up to make porridge or ground even finer to make flour for bread. It was also used to make a weak beer. Most people only ate meat on special occasions. Almost everyone drank milk or beer, especially if they did not live close to a source of fresh water.

The women of the family cooked over an open fire, usually outside. In the rainy season they cooked in a special kitchen hut. They did not cook in their homes because they were afraid of starting a fire. Each village had at least one large bread oven, which the women used to bake bread.

A West African family would have plenty of jars for storing food. They were often decorated.

Families

West Africans lived in large family groups. Marriages were arranged by the families. The wife usually went to live with her husband's family. The husband's family paid a "bride price," usually cattle or cloth, for the wife. The amount of the bride price depended on how rich the families were.

Everyone living in the village was expected to help everyone else. In each compound, the children called all old women "grandmother" and all old men "grandfather." They all called each other "brother" and "sister."

Even when family members died, West Africans believed their **spirits** lived on. Figurines buried in graves linked the living with the spirit of the person who had died.

Masks played an important part in the ceremonies of the West African kingdoms.

Men and women lived very separate lives. Men worked together, joked together, and ate together. The women worked and ate with the children. There were special **ceremonies** for when a boy was old enough to stop living like a child and could join the men. Boys learned the same trade as their fathers and uncles, and they had to learn the secret **rituals** of songs and dances that each trade had. Girls learned how to run a home.

Everyone joined together for weddings, funerals, and rituals held at special times, such as **harvest** time. Some of these **festivals** lasted for days, with a lot of singing, dancing, eating, and drinking.

Clothes

Gold jewelry was one of the ways that people could show their wealth and importance. This woman is wearing huge gold earrings.

The weather in West Africa was very hot, even during the rainy season, but the nights could get cold sometimes. Most of the time, though, people did not need to wear clothes to keep warm. The earliest West Africans went naked, with maybe an animal skin as a cloak in the coldest weather.

Later, clothes came to be a way of showing importance and wealth. There was a rule in some kingdoms that only the king could wear sandals. Unlike everyone else, he was too important to have his feet touch the ground. People, especially in the cities, also stared to wear more clothes. They did so as they met other peoples who wore more clothes, such as **Muslim** traders from the north.

Because the weather in West Africa was so warm, most people just wore a simple apron and no shoes. The woman is carrying a baby in a cloth sling.

When West African traders began to meet traders from North Africa face to face, many of them began to dress in the same way. This West African trader is wearing a long robe like those worn by traders from across the Sahara.

A king would wear sandals, an elegant tunic, and a skullcap. His servant wears a plain apron and carries a shade to protect the king from the sun.

Writing and Storytelling

The people of West Africa had a spoken language, but they did not believe in writing things down at first. For many years they passed on stories and knowledge **orally**.

Some people enjoyed riddles and **proverbs** that anyone could tell. But there were storytellers called **griots** whose job it was to remember and pass on the important stories of each group of people. Often they would tell their stories to music, playing a drum or stringed instrument while they spoke. They told the stories at **rituals**, often with the help of other people acting out the story with masks and dancing.

Griots are still an important part of West African culture. A female griot is called a griotte.

This book was found in Tombouctou. It is written in Arabic, the main language of many Muslims.

While the West Africans did not have a tradition of writing things down, the North African **Muslims** they traded with did. Muslim travelers wrote the only descriptions we have of Tombouctou and Djenné at the time. They also wrote down the names of the rulers and their laws and customs.

As West African rulers became Muslim, they needed to read the **Qu'ran** and obey Muslim laws. To do this they had to learn to read and write. Teachers came to the cities from North Africa, and schools and **universities** sprang up.

Modern West Africa

Some of the photographs in this book show modern West Africa. This is because the people there do many things in the same way as their ancestors from the old kingdoms of Ghana, Mali, and Songhai. Farmers grow similar crops in similar ways. Homes in the countryside are still built using similar materials to cope with a similar climate. Storytellers and **griots** still tell the same stories.

Not everything is unchanged. The cities have changed the most. They have electricity, cars, telephones, and other modern inventions.

Huge slabs of salt are for sale at a large market. Salt is still one of the main trade goods in West Africa.

Glossary

ceremony set of acts with religious meaning

court king or queen and their advisors

diviner person who tells ordinary people how to please the gods

festival time of celebration

griot West African storyteller and musician

harvest season when crops are gathered; or, to gather a crop

mosque Muslim temple

Muslim member of a religious group that follows the teachings of Muhammed

offering something given to a god

official person who runs a country for the ruler

oral spoken, not written

plaza large open square in the center of a city or town

proverb wise saying

Qu'ran Muslim holy book

ritual ceremony that is done the same way every time

slave person belonging to someone else who is forced to work without pay

spirit being that cannot be seen

temple building for religious worship

university high-level school

Find Out More

Books

Armentrout, David and Patricia. *Ghana, Mali, Songhay.* Vero Beach, Fla.: Rourke, 2003.

Barr, Gary. *History and Activities of the West African Kingdoms.* Chicago: Heinemann Library, 2007.

Reece, Katherine E. *West African Kingdoms: Empires of Gold and Trade.* Vero Beach, Fla.: Rourke, 2006.

Websites

www.bbc.co.uk/worldservice/africa/features/storyofafrica/index_section4.shtml. A BBC website that explores the "Story of Africa".

www.history.com/classroom/unesco/timbuktu.html. Learn about West African kingdoms through the city of Timbuktu (Tombouctou).

Index

DUNCAN & DOLORES

BY BARBARA SAMUELS

A TRUMPET CLUB SPECIAL EDITION

Published by The Trumpet Club
666 Fifth Avenue, New York, New York 10103

ISBN: 0-440-84451-7

This edition published by arrangement with
Macmillan Publishing Company
Printed in the United States of America
October 1991

10 9 8 7 6 5 4 3 2 1

UPC

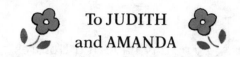

To JUDITH
and AMANDA

One day Faye and Dolores
saw a sign:

NEEDS A HOME
4 YEARS OLD - HIS NAME
IS DUNCAN.

"He's cute," said Dolores, "and he's
just my age. I want a cat like that."

"But animals run away from you, Dolores."
"I want that cat," said Dolores.
"Poor Duncan," sighed Faye.

The Next Day ...

Duncan was delivered in a case.
"Now you are my cat," said Dolores,
"and you will come out and play with me."

Duncan shot out of the case and disappeared under
a cabinet.

"Oh dear, it's starting already," said Faye.

Later That Night...

"Come to bed, Dolores."
"I'm going to sit here till Duncan comes out."
"Just leave some food by the cabinet. He'll
come out when he's ready," said Faye.

"Okay, but I'll leave him this note
so he'll know where I am."

"Oh, brother," said Faye.

Two Days Later...

"I'm so glad you finally came out, Duncan.
Now we can play dress up."

"Cats don't play dress up," said Faye.

"Duncan does. Today I will wear a beautiful
cape and he can wear this lovely hat."

Duncan didn't want to play dress up.

"I understand, Duncan. You would rather
do tricks. I will throw this ball and you
will bring it back to me. *Go get it, Duncan!*"

Duncan didn't want to do tricks.

"Here, Duncan," called Faye softly, "you
don't have to do tricks." Duncan walked
over to Faye and sat in her lap.

The Next Morning...

"Duncan doesn't like me," said Dolores.
"He likes you better than me."

"I think he's afraid of you," said Faye.

"Duncan afraid of me, how silly!"

"You're not afraid of me, are you, Duncan?"

"How come you always play with Faye?"

"You never play with me!"

"It isn't fair!"

"It would be a lot quieter around here if
you'd leave that poor cat alone," Faye grumbled.

"That's fine with me," said Dolores. "I have
better things to do than chase that fat cat."

Dolores made a hiding place with
chairs and an old blanket.

Then she had tea with Martha and Mabel.
She did not ask Duncan to join them.

After tea she played the piano
and refused to notice Duncan.

And when she took her nap she hugged
her teddy bear, not Duncan.

Later That Day…

Duncan rolled the paintbrush toward
Dolores. It stopped at her feet.

"Why, thank you, Duncan," said Dolores.
Duncan purred softly.

That Night...

"Duncan sat on my easel today," said Dolores.
"Really," said Faye.

"Then he brought me my paintbrush."
"That's nice," said Faye.

"Look, Faye," whispered Dolores,
"look at Duncan...."

"His chin is on my neck and it tickles....Faye,"

"Uh-oh!"